*To my loving wife, Maureen,*
*who through the years has encouraged and*
*supported my hobby of "taking pictures."*

# MUSKOKA

## CHANGE OF SEASONS

PHOTOGRAPHS BY
NORRIS E. HUNT

THE ONTARIO HISTORICAL SOCIETY

Published by the Town of Huntsville in co-operation with Heritage Huntsville
through a generous donation by Dr. Norris E. Hunt.

Distributed by Fox Meadow Creations
Box 5401, Huntsville, Ontario P1H 2K7
www.foxmeadowbooks.com / Tel. 705-788-0469

*Cataloguing in Publication Data*

Hunt, Norris E.
Muskoka : change of seasons / Photographs by Norris E. Hunt.

ISBN 0-9734434-0-5

1. Muskoka (Ont.) — Pictorial works. I. Title.

FC 3095 M88D48 2003     971.3'1604'0222

Book designed and typeset by Fox Meadow Creations
Printed and bound in Canada by Friesens
Typeface is Eplica

TITLE PAGE  *View down Peninsula Lake from the summit of Wolf Mountain.*

FRONT COVER *(main picture)*  *Sunset over Fairy Lake.*

BACK COVER *(main picture)*  *The Muskoka Loppet, Mary Lake.*

# FOREWORD

Heritage Huntsville is proud to be associated with this splendid book of Muskoka photographs, the work of Dr. Norris Hunt, a resident of Huntsville for many years.

Dr. Hunt's interest in photography has led to many contributions to the people of Huntsville. He has been a leading member of the local Camera Club. For many years his photographs have enhanced the patient rooms of the Huntsville and District Memorial Hospital. Working with his wife, Maureen, he has taken hundreds of photographs of buildings in and around Huntsville, which have helped us all to appreciate our built heritage.

The outstanding pictures collected in this volume include many of Dr. Hunt's personal favourites. They attest to his deep love for the Muskoka landscape and the activities of the people in this special place in Canada. This book is another contribution to us all, letting us see through the eyes of an artist the beauty of our world.

Elspeth Hogg
Heritage Huntsville

*Edge of the pond, January.*

# A VIEW OF MUSKOKA

Words cannot begin to describe the scenic splendour of Ontario's Muskoka District, which has been attracting visitors for a hundred and forty years now. Myriad sparkling lakes, placid rivers, thundering waterfalls, rolling hills carpeted with hardwood forests, rocky shores clad in pine—not only does the variety of the landscape impress, but each of the four seasons brings its own distinct character, providing an almost limitless visual spectrum.

Situated on the southern edge of the rugged precambrian Canadian Shield between Georgian Bay and Algonquin Park, Muskoka lies in the transition zone between the northern boreal forests and the southern hardwoods. Here may be found scenes distinctly northern in flavour, and close by, even visible from the same vantage point, landscapes suggestive of a locale much farther south.

Despite the rocky underpinnings of the district, agriculture was the motive when the region was opened for pioneer settlement in the 1860s. Farmers did eke out a living on pockets of arable land between the hills, but the main industry for many years was forestry as lumbermen stalked the giant white pines and sent logs tumbling down the rivers to the sawmills. Picturesque remnants of the pioneer farming era, however, still dot the landscape.

Accessible by rail after 1875, and boasting fleets of steamboats plying the large lake systems, Muskoka with its natural beauty and recreational opportunities was virtually assured its status as Ontario's summer vacation destination. Resorts steadily more grand sprang up on the shores of the major lakes in the late nineteenth and early twentieth centuries; millionaires' summer mansions and ordinary folks' cottages took their place amongst the pine, oak, maple and birch along the shores.

Not surprisingly, Muskoka has inspired generations of artists and photographers. Guidebooks from the 1870s and 1880s display magnificent wood engravings, often romanticized, of Muskoka lake and waterfall scenes. Some members of the Group of Seven painted in Muskoka, and many artists today have made the district their home. In recent years a number of lavish full-colour coffee-table books of Muskoka scenes have appeared on the market.

Dr. Norris E. Hunt—"Joe" to those who know him—was immediately enchanted by the Muskoka landscape when he moved to the Huntsville area with his wife, Maureen, and children in 1969. Already an accomplished hobby photographer, he found the combination of the wonderful natural surroundings and the relics of Muskoka's cultural heritage an unbeatable inspiration to continue to hone his artist's eye behind the lens of the camera.

Dr. Hunt attributes his special interest in the beauty around him, and in capturing it on film, in part to his experiences during World War II. A Spitfire fighter pilot, he was shot down over France in 1942 and spent three years in a German prisoner-of-war camp. For the duration of his incarceration, his view was limited to guard towers, barbed wire, and the desolate scrub pine forest of the remote location. Deprived of anything approaching beauty, he would take special pleasure from it when he was freed.

Over the years, on excursions around Muskoka, he recorded what he considered artistically and historically interesting. Encompassing scenic panoramas, wildflowers, old farm buildings, people engaged in enjoying everything the outdoors has to offer, in all seasons of the year, his images reflect an eclectic appreciation for his surroundings. With wife Maureen closely involved for many years in developing the Muskoka Pioneer Village at Huntsville, naturally Dr. Hunt also found rich subject matter for his camera amongst that collection of historic buildings.

It was never Dr. Hunt's intention to take photographs specifically to publish commercially in a book. This volume, a collection of about ninety of his images, contains a cross-section of the themes he found it personally pleasurable to record over the years. Out of the many possible ways of organizing them, it was decided to present them in order of the seasons—Nature's own progression. While autumn is particularly well represented—who can resist Muskoka's stunning fall foliage?—the large number of colourful winter scenes will delight the many who normally only see Muskoka in summer or autumn; and spring, in practical terms a very short season of about six weeks and again often neglected, has surprising variety and beauty.

Since Dr. Hunt resides in Huntsville, the majority of his images are of scenes throughout the highlands of northeastern Muskoka—Fairy, Peninsula and Mary lakes, Arrowhead Park, the Oxtongue River. This splendid area of lofty rolling hills, wild rivers, and enchanting lakes is not so well represented in other photographic collections of the district, which tend to concentrate on the Muskoka Lakes. This book, then, provides a fresh and different view of Muskoka.

We begin Dr. Hunt's photographic explorations in late spring with the forests alive with the bursting of new growth.

*Dense patches of sun-loving white trillium briefly turn the floor of hardwood forests snow white again just before the tree leaves fully unfurl and plunge the understorey into deep shade. Although spring officially ends at the solstice in June, Muskoka actually dons its summer cloak with the leaf-out in May.*

*"One Tree" Island in Fairy Lake boasts several trees now, but hasn't lost any of its photogenic qualities. At one time it supported a single pine tree.*

*The sun sinks behind the distinctive whale-back hills that lend Fairy Lake much of its charm.*
*The enchanting scenery prompted geologist Alexander Murray to give the lake its name*
*on a canoe expedition through Muskoka in 1853.*

*"Mmmmm! They all look so good!" The C.W. Hay general store at Muskoka Pioneer Village, Huntsville.*

FACING PAGE *Early morning reflections on the North Muskoka River in downtown Huntsville.*

*A glorious summer day along the canal between Fairy and Peninsula lakes.*

FACING PAGE *Lupins and yellow lilies.*

*Groves of lofty white pine stand sentinel behind this lakeside retreat.*

*They're not indigenous to Muskoka, but sunflowers certainly evoke the summer feeling.*

*The water-lily, an elegant resident of ponds and shallow corners of lakes and streams in Muskoka.*

FACING PAGE *With a colourful splash, participants in a Muskoka Triathlon hit the waters of Peninsula Lake.*

*One can imagine the farmer has gotten off his tractor for a minute to lie in the daisies to soak up this pastoral scene. The crop here, typical in Muskoka today, is hay.*

FACING PAGE *Sunrise over Fairy Lake from The Lookout at Huntsville.*

*"Les Voyageurs" enjoy an excursion on Lake Vernon, while on the facing page the* RMS *Segwun, oldest operating steamboat in North America (since 1887), gets up steam at the wharf at Windermere, Lake Rosseau.*

*Mahogany motor launch at Port Carling. Hundreds of the sleek craft were once manufactured by Muskoka boat builders; many, lovingly maintained or restored, still cruise area lakes.*

FACING PAGE *The delicate columbine is a member of the buttercup family.*

*Keeping the home fires burning at the Spence Inn, Muskoka Pioneer Village.*

FACING PAGE *Misty morning with moon over hayfield.*

*Two symbols of an earlier era in Muskoka. A sleek mahogany launch skims across Lake Rosseau in front of Windermere House, one of the grand old resorts of the district (established in the 1870s).*

FACING PAGE *Muskoka sunset.*

*Misty morning on the links near the canal between Fairy and Peninsula lakes. Muskoka's rugged terrain has provided exciting possibilities for golf course designers—and scenic challenges for golfers.*

FACING PAGE *Reliving the past at Muskoka Pioneer Village, Huntsville.*

The smooth, gently sloping rocks of Port Sydney Falls on the North Muskoka River
have attracted "sliders" for more than a century.

FACING PAGE  *Muskoka's pioneers planted apple trees, and many an old orchard still faithfully bears fruit.
By the time the apples fully ripen, summer is sliding into autumn.*

*A hazy late September day along Brown's Road, near Huntsville.*
*The maples are reaching their most brilliant.*

FACING PAGE *Old boardwalk at Cann Lake, Muskoka Pioneer Village.*
*Lots of green in the woods yet, but also unmistakable signs that autumn has begun.*

*Sunday best at Muskoka Pioneer Village in September.*

FACING PAGE  *A young sugar maple sends a crimson flame skyward amid this grove of birch and aspen on a sand plain bordering Arrowhead Lake in Arrowhead Provincial Park.*

*A happy Muskoka couple.*

FACING PAGE *Leaf artistry.*

*Along the Oxtongue Rapids, Oxtongue River.*

FACING PAGE  *The brilliant oranges and reds of the maples seem like a fire amongst the dark pines and the still-green birch and aspen as the "maple" phase of fall colour reaches its peak.*

*The Oxtongue Rupids.*

FACING PAGE *Dropping nearly 50 feet over a cliff, High Falls on the North Muskoka River is one of Muskoka's most impressive cataracts.*

*Sometimes it seems Mother Nature has squeezed primary colours straight from the tube.*

FACING PAGE *Interior of the woods through the gnarled limbs of a black cherry.*

*Scenes at the Brunel Lock, North Muskoka River near Huntsville.*

*Sunset over the hills at Hunter's Bay, Huntsville.*


*FACING PAGE  Beech tree overhanging the Oxtongue Rapids.*

*The Big East River valley can always be counted on for its splendid display of fall colours.*

FACING PAGE  *Glowing reflections.*

*October—the water looks cold! This is the beach at Arrowhead Lake, Arrowhead Provincial Park.*

FACING PAGE *The russet brown of the red oak and golden yellow of aspen reserve their rich display for mid-October, after the more flamboyant maples have dropped their flaming foliage.*

*"Hmm, that looks like a good apple."* The Hay store, at Muskoka Pioneer Village,
was originally located in the village of Falkenburg, near Bracebridge.

*A struggling red maple ekes a living from moisture and nutrients*
*in a crevice on this rocky hilltop.*

*Birches behind the Spence Inn, Muskoka Pioneer Village. The Inn once was a stopping place on the Nipissing Colonization Road that ran from Lake Rosseau to Lake Nipissing.*

FACING PAGE *Nights are getting cold—better get those tomatoes in. Muskoka Pioneer Village.*

*A calm morning at Cann Lake, Huntsville.*
*The tamarack have turned their smoky late autumn gold and will soon shed their needles.*

*Frosty fall morning.*

*A ride in the highlands near Peninsula Lake on a gorgeous fall afternoon.*

FACING PAGE *Fairy Lake from The Lookout at Huntsville. The red oak (foreground) can display a variety of colours ranging from yellow-brown through red to deep red-brown.*

*Canoeing on the Little East River, Arrowhead Provincial Park, in October.*

FACING PAGE *An early dusting of snow—a reminder that winter is just around the corner.*

*It was cold last night!*

FACING PAGE *First snow reflections, Cann Lake, Huntsville.*

*End of season.*

*In days gone by a sturdy team like this would be engaged in hauling sleigh-loads of pine logs out of the woods.*

FACING PAGE *Early winter panorama of parts of Fairy and Peninsula lakes from a hilltop at Grandview.*

*Cross-country skiing in Arrowhead Provincial Park.*

FACING PAGE *Winter shadow patterns.*

*Shadow patterns on snow.*

FACING PAGE *"Bean-can" curling on Cann Lake at Muskoka Pioneer Village.*

*Old fields near Huntsville.*

FACING PAGE *Making a "telemark" turn on cross-country skis!*
*Both alpine and cross-country skiing have been popular activities in Muskoka over the years. During the 1930s and 1940s Huntsville boasted one of the world's most thrilling ski jumps, on Mica Mine Hill beside Fairy Lake.*

*The original Christ Church (Anglican) at Port Sydney, built in the 1870s.*

FACING PAGE *A Victorian Christmas at the Hill House, Muskoka Pioneer Village.*

*Hitting the snowmobile trails between Fairy and Peninsula lakes.*

FACING PAGE *Participants in the Muskoka Loppet tackle a hill at the edge of Mary Lake.*

*I bet that mug of cocoa tastes good!*

*Light and shadow on the Oxtongue River.*

*The family that built this pioneer homestead in northern Muskoka had its dreams.*

FACING PAGE  *The splendid Queen Anne style "Hart House" overlooks the Huntsville waterfront. It was constructed in 1893-4 for Dr. J.W. Hart, who had started Huntsville's first hospital in 1886.*

*After a long cold winter, the call "sap's running" is welcome—especially for those with a sweet tooth!*
*The scenes on these pages and the following two are at sugar bushes near Huntsville,*
*including that at Muskoka Pioneer Village.*

*Boil maple syrup until really thick, pour out on fresh cold snow, and … maple taffy!*

*Off on a spring fishing trip. Good luck, fellows!*

FACING PAGE *Spring break-up on Fairy Lake.*
*A good wind will quickly remove these fragile remnants of winter ice.*

*Even smaller streams in Muskoka thunder with spring meltwaters.*

*Fresh from the river or lake.*

*A tinge of fresh green on the trees at Fairy Lake (facing page), and the trilliums again—here the less common but beautiful painted trillium—and we've come full circle on this photographic tour of the seasons in Muskoka.*

PHOTO BY KIM FELLOWS

*For their assistance and encouragement over the course of this book project, I would like to thank Judith Ruan of The Bookcase, Elspeth Hogg of Heritage Huntsville, Hugh Mackenzie, Mayor of Huntsville, and Gary Long of Fox Meadow Creations. Doug Millikin, Peter and Nick Musters, Ian McTavish, Sandy Raven, Jon Snelson, and Jim Bartlett of Cavalcade Color Lab, helped me through the intricacies in the new (for me) computer process of producing colour prints of my images. I must also thank my wife, Maureen, for her support and patience when I frequently got carried away and "just a quick shot" somehow got extended. This project has truly been a labour of love.*

Joe Hunt